Contents

T5-DHU-974

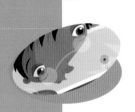

Chapter 1

Thump! Thump! Thump!

"Thump!"

Tim wakes up. Saturday! A fun day. In the fridge is the gelatin he made last night. Tim loves gelatin. This is going to be a great day.

"Thump!"

Tim frowns. What is that?

"Thump!"

It's coming from the closet. Tim creeps over and slides the door open. A tiny purple alien steps out and pokes Tim on the foot.

"Take me to your weader!"

Tim jumps back on the bed. The alien is only as big as a teddy bear, but he has a funny-looking wand pointed at Tim.

"Wha . . . what?" Tim asks.

"Take me to your weader!" the alien squeaks.

"My weader?"

"Your weader! Your weader!" The alien looks
at a tiny screen on his third arm. "I am
taking over your pwanet. Give up!"

"My pwanet?" Tim asks.

Chapter 2

Taking Over

"Give up!" the alien shouts.

"But you're so little," Tim says.

The alien frowns with two of his three foreheads.

"Me NOT wittle!" He points his wand. A beam of light shoots out and zaps Tim on the elbow.

"Hee-hee! It feels like lots of tickling fingers."

The alien looks at his wand. He holds it with one of his three hands and points it again. This time it tickles Tim's ankle.

"Hey! Stop it!" Tim jumps off the bed, bends down, and pulls the wand from the alien. "Stop it! It tickles!"

The alien looks up at Tim with three, very surprised, round eyes.

He turns a darker shade of purple and jumps onto Tim's foot.

The alien wraps two of his arms around Tim's ankles. Then he tickles Tim's leg with his third arm. "Give up!"

Tim hops around the room, shaking his foot. "Get off!"

The alien clings on. "Your pwanet is taken over!" the alien squeaks. Steam begins to pour from the ears on his knees.

"How many of you are there?" Tim asks.

The alien stops hitting Tim. "One."

Tim stops hopping and laughs. "One? You?
But you're too little."

"Me not wittle. Give up!"

"No!" laughs Tim.

"No?"

Tim's cat, Rusty, walks into the room.
The alien jumps off Tim's foot and runs to
the cat.

"Take me to your weader!"

Rusty purrs and rubs her head on the alien's purple tummy. The alien's three eyes bulge.

"She doesn't have a leader. She is a cat. Look, what's your name?" Tim asks.

"Gweep."

"Well, Gweep, you can't take over this planet."

Gweep sits down and rubs his three foreheads with two of his hands. "Me in twouble. Me in BIG twouble."

"Why?" asks Tim as he sits down beside Gweep.

"This is the sixth pwanet me
NOT take over," Gweep moans.

"Is taking over planets your job?"

"Yes. This meant to be easy pwanet.
You meant to be swime. Not big and hopping
and saying no." Gweep rubs his foreheads
again.

Chapter 3

Toothpicks

"Sorry," Tim says, "I'm not slime."

Gweep looks sad. "If you reawwy sowwy, you talk to boss of Gweep. You say, 'Gweep take over my pwanet. He very good at it.' Then boss not stuff me and use me for footrest."

"Will he really do that?" Tim asks.

"No — maybe just chop me up and use bones for toothpicks," Gweep says sadly.

"Oh well, I guess I could say that you took over my pwan . . . I mean planet."

"Gweep be vewy happy if you do. Gweep go
away to take over other pwanet. Small one
nearby is made of cheese. Cheese not say no."

Tim shrugs. "OK. I want you to be very
happy."

Gweep jumps up and runs to the closet. He pushes aside some fallen clothes. There stands a shiny spaceship, shaped like an upside down ice cream cone.

Gweep pulls open a small door. "Come in."

Tim shakes his head. "I can't fit in there."

Gweep frowns with all three of his foreheads. "You not even twy!"

"Try? I'm too big!" Tim laughs.

"Maybe I just take your head," says Gweep.

"No!"

"Then I take cat. Cat not big. I tell my weader I take over cat."

"No — you can't take my cat. Wait here," says Tim. "I have an idea."

Chapter 4

Green Slime

Tim runs down to the kitchen and grabs the lime gelatin from the fridge. He takes it back to the odd little alien. Gweep is busy trying to push the cat through the tiny door of his spaceship.

"Stop that! You're not taking Rusty," Tim gasps. "Here is some slime instead."

Gweep looks in the bowl. "This bad."

Tim looks at the yummy, wobbly, green gelatin. "It's really very nice."

Tears form in Gweep's three round eyes. "It saying no!"

Tim pats Gweep on his middle shoulder. "The slime isn't saying no. It's shaking because it's so scared of you. Take it back to your leader and show him. Tell your leader you have taken over all the gel . . . slime on Earth."

"Is it scared?" Gweep smiles. "Of me?"

"Yes," Tim answers.

Gweep laughs. He snatches the bowl of gelatin, runs into his spaceship, and slams the door. The closet rumbles and shakes. With a puff of smoke, the spaceship is gone.

27

All week Tim wonders about Gweep. What happened to him? Where did he go? Did he get made into toothpicks?

On Friday, Tim helps his mom unpack the shopping. She has bought a new type of gelatin. Tim smiles as he reads the label.

Glossary

alien
creature from outer space

bulge
stick out

footrest
low stool where you rest your feet

galactic
relating to a galaxy or a large star system

gelatin
soft, sweet food that wobbles

purr
low noise made by a
happy cat

slime
thin, sticky, slippery mud

toothpicks
small pointed sticks used to
remove food from teeth

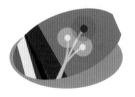

wand
a pointer that's magic

Bren MacDibble

I love "Doctor! Doctor!" jokes. Not only are the jokes funny, but they are quick to tell. This is important for someone who can only keep a straight face for a couple of seconds. It's hard to finish a joke when you're giggling!

Doctor! Doctor! I feel like I'm invisible!
Who said that?

Doctor! Doctor! I think I'm turning into a dog!
Sit on the couch and tell me all about it.
I can't. I'm not allowed up on the couch!

Doctor! Doctor! My sister thinks she's an elevator!
Well, tell her to come in.
I can't! She doesn't stop at this floor!

Nathan Jurevicius

FOUR STEPS TO FUN

1. Find a sleepy cat.

2. Get an old record player.

3. Find an old record.*

4. Watch your cat go crazy!

*Ask someone old, like your mom or dad!

Take Me to Your Leader!

by Bren MacDibble

illustrated by Nathan Jurevicius

Harcourt Achieve

Rigby • Saxon • Steck-Vaughn

www.HarcourtAchieve.com
1.800.531.5015

Characters

Tim

Gweep

Rusty